Cupcakes Fo

40 Exceptional Cupcake Recipes to make you Feel Blessed

BY

MOLLY MILLS

Copyright © 2019 by Molly Mills

License Notes

No part of this book may be copied, replicated, distributed, sold or shared without the express and written consent of the Author.

The ideas expressed in the book are for entertainment purposes. The Reader assumes all risk when following any guidelines and the Author accepts no responsibility if damages occur due to actions taken by the Reader.

An Amazing Offer for Buying My Book!

Thank you very much for purchasing my books! As a token of my appreciation, I would like to extend an amazing offer to you! When you have subscribed with your e-mail address, you will have the opportunity to get free and discounted e-books that will show up in your inbox daily. You will also receive reminders before an offer expires so you never miss out. With just little effort on your part, you will have access to the newest and most informative books at your fingertips. This is all part of the VIP treatment when you subscribe below.

SIGN ME UP: *https://molly.gr8.com*

Table of Contents

Chapter I - Chocolate Cupcakes 8

    Recipe 1: Triple Choc Cupcakes 9

    Recipe 2: Rocky Road Cupcakes 13

    Recipe 3: Peanut Butter and Chocolate Cupcakes 17

    Recipe 4: Black Forest Gateau Cupcakes 21

    Recipe 5: White Chocolate and Pistachio Cupcakes..... 25

    Recipe 6: Death by Chocolate Cupcakes 29

    Recipe 7: S'more Cupcakes 33

    Recipe 8: Jaffa Cupcakes 37

    Recipe 9: Salted Caramel and Chocolate Cupcakes...... 41

    Recipe 10: Mint Chocolate Cupcakes 44

Chapter II - Fruit Cupcakes.. 47

    Recipe 11: Watermelon Cupcakes 48

Recipe 12: Banoffee Pie Cupcakes 52

Recipe 13: Very Berry Cupcakes 55

Recipe 14: Blueberry 'Muffin' Cupcakes 59

Recipe 15: Strawberries and Cream Cupcakes 63

Recipe 16: Coconut Lime Cupcakes 66

Recipe 17: Raspberry and White Chocolate Cupcakes . 70

Recipe 18: Lemon Meringue Pie Cupcakes 73

Recipe 19: Passionfruit Cheesecake Cupcakes 77

Recipe 20: Mango and Vanilla Cupcakes 81

Chapter III - Vegan/Gluten Free Cupcakes 84

Recipe 21: Vegan Vanilla Cupcakes 85

Recipe 22: Carrot and Vanilla Cupcakes 88

Recipe 23: Strawberry Beet Cupcakes 92

Recipe 24: Chocolate Cupcakes 96

Recipe 25: Snickerdoodle Cupcakes 100

Recipe 26: Chocolate Chip Cupcakes 103

Recipe 27: Peach and Honey Buttercream Cupcakes . 106

Recipe 28: Funfetti Cupcakes 109

Recipe 29: Natural Red Velvet Cupcakes 112

Recipe 30: Green Tea, Pecan, and Salted Caramel Cupcakes 115

Chapter IV - Over 21s Cupcakes 118

Recipe 31: Tiramisu Cupcakes.................................... 119

Recipe 32: Cosmopolitan Cupcakes............................ 123

Recipe 33: Spiced Sangria Cupcakes 127

Recipe 34: Gin and Tonic Cupcakes 130

Recipe 35: Rum and Raisin... 134

Recipe 36: Colleen's Irish Coffee Cupcakes............... 137

Recipe 37: Pink Champagne Cupcakes....................... 140

Recipe 38: Margarita Cupcakes 143

Recipe 39: Pina Colada Cupcakes 147

Recipe 40: Mojito Cupcakes 151

About the Author 155

Don't Miss Out! 157

Chapter I - Chocolate Cupcakes

AAAAAAAAAAAAAAAAAAAAAAAAAAAAAAAAAAAAAAAAAA

Recipe 1: Triple Choc Cupcakes

Milk, white and dark chocolate come together to make these delicious cocoa-packed cupcakes. The addition of coffee in this recipe makes for an exceedingly rich and intense chocolate sponge.

Yield: 18

Preparation Time: 20mins

Total Cooking Time: 20mins

List of Ingredients:

Cupcakes:

- 1 cup all-purpose flour
- 1 cup sugar
- ⅔ cup cocoa powder (unsweetened)
- 1 teaspoon baking soda
- ½ teaspoons salt
- ½ cup buttermilk
- 1 teaspoon baking powder
- 2 tablespoons Greek yogurt
- ⅓ cup oil
- ½ tablespoons vanilla extract
- ½ cup espresso (hot)

Frosting:

- 2 cups cream cheese (softened)
- 1 cup confectioner's sugar
- 3/8 cup white chocolate (melted and cooled)
- 1/8 cup milk chocolate (melted and cooled)
- 1½ cups whipping cream (cold)
- Dark chocolate (grated)

AA

Instructions:

1. Preheat oven to 350 degrees F.

2. Mix dry ingredients together in a large bowl.

3. In a separate bowl, use an electric whisk to mix the buttermilk, egg, yogurt, vanilla, and oil.

4. Add the dry ingredients to the wet, little by little, mixing continuously.

5. Add in the coffee and stir well to combine.

6. Fill each cupcake case with the mixture until 1/2 full and smooth the surface of each with the back of a spoon. Bake for approximately 20 minutes. Remove the cupcakes from the baking tin and place on a wire rack to cool.

7. To prepare the frosting, mix confectioner's sugar and cream cheese, until smooth.

8. Pour the melted white and milk chocolate into the cream cheese mix and whisk well.

9. In another bowl, whip the cream until stiff peaks are formed.

10. Combine the whipped cream and cream cheese mixtures, folding gently.

11. Pipe the cooled cupcakes with the frosting and decorate with a sprinkling of grated dark chocolate.

Recipe 2: Rocky Road Cupcakes

Rocky road was America's bestselling ice cream flavor, and it's easy to see why! With a little bit of everything, from peanuts to mini marshmallows, these cupcakes have something for everyone.

Yield: 12

Preparation Time: 1h

Total Cooking Time: 30mins

List of Ingredients:

Cupcakes:

- ¼ cup oil
- 4 tablespoons unsalted butter
- ½ cup water
- 1 cup sugar
- 1 cup all-purpose flour
- ¼ cup and 2 tablespoons cocoa powder (unsweetened)
- ¼ teaspoons salt
- ¾ teaspoons baking soda
- 1 egg
- ¼ cup buttermilk
- 1 teaspoon vanilla extract
- ¼ cup oil

Frosting and Toppings:

- ½ cup heavy cream
- 3 tablespoons unsalted butter
- 1 tablespoon light corn syrup
- Pinch of salt
- 1 cup bittersweet chocolate (chopped)
- Baby marshmallows
- Salted peanuts (chopped)
- Mini chocolate chips

Instructions:

1. Preheat oven to 350 degrees F.

2. In a saucepan over low heat, melt oil and butter.

3. In a mixing bowl, sift together sugar, flour, cocoa powder, salt, and baking soda. Pour in the melted butter and blend with an electric whisk. Add in the egg, buttermilk, and vanilla, and mix until all ingredients are well combined.

4. Fill each cupcake case with the mixture until 3/4 full and smooth the surface of each with the back of a spoon. Bake 25 minutes. Remove the cupcakes from the baking tin and place on a wire rack to cool.

5. In the meantime, use a double boiler to melt together cream, butter, corn syrup and salt and pour over the chocolate pieces. Set aside for 5 minutes then mix with a fork until smooth. Leave the mixture to stand for 1 hour until it is firm enough to be piped.

6. Fold the marshmallows, peanuts and choc chips into the frosting and frost the cupcakes.

Recipe 3: Peanut Butter and Chocolate Cupcakes

Just like a good PB&J sandwich, this recipe strikes the perfect balance between sweet and salty. The peanut butter in this recipe is used as a scrumptious gooey filling.

Yield: 12

Preparation Time: 30mins

Total Cooking Time: 25mins

List of Ingredients:

Filling:

- ¾ cup full-fat cream cheese (softened)
- ¼ cup smooth peanut butter
- 2 tablespoons sugar
- 1 tablespoon milk

Cupcakes:

- 2 cups white sugar
- 1¾ cups flour (all-purpose)
- ½ cup cocoa powder
- 1 teaspoon salt
- 1½ teaspoons baking powder
- ¼ teaspoons baking soda
- 3 small eggs
- 1 cup water
- 1 cup milk
- ½ cup oil

AAAAAAAAAAAAAAAAAAAAAAAAAAAAAAAAAAAAAAAAAAAAAAAA

Instructions:

1. First, prepare the filling. Mix the cream cheese, peanut butter, sugar, and milk. Set to one side until needed later.

2. In a mixing bowl, sift together the sugar, cocoa powder, flour, salt, baking powder, and soda.

3. In a separate bowl, whisk together the eggs, water, milk, and oil.

4. Slowly pour the wet ingredients into the dry ingredients, whisking continuously. The batter will be somewhat thin/runny.

5. Fill each cupcake case with the mixture until 1/2 full. Drop a spoonful of peanut butter filling into the center of the batter and top with more cake mix. Smooth the surface of each with the back of a spoon. Bake for approximately 27 minutes, or until a cocktail stick inserted into the cupcake (avoid the peanut butter) comes out clean. Remove the cupcakes from the baking tin and place on a wire rack to cool.

6. In the meantime, mix all frosting ingredients until well combined.

7. Pipe the cooled cupcakes with the frosting.

Recipe 4: Black Forest Gateau Cupcakes

Rich chocolate sponge, whipped cream topping and an 'oh so sweet' surprise cherry filling. Perfect for dessert, these decadent little cupcakes are impossible to say no to.

Yield: 12

Preparation Time: 30mins

Total Cooking Time: 20mins

List of Ingredients:

Cupcake:

- ⅓ cup cocoa powder (unsweetened)
- ¾ cup bittersweet chocolate (finely chopped)
- ¾ water (hot)
- ¾ cup sugar
- ¾ cup bread flour
- ½ teaspoons salt
- ½ teaspoons baking soda
- 3 small eggs
- ¼ cup and 2 tablespoons canola oil
- 1½ vanilla extract
- 2 teaspoons white vinegar

Filling:

- 1¼ cups pie filling (preferably cherry, strawberry/raspberry is also fine)

Topping:

- 1½ cups heavy cream
- ¼ cup sugar
- Dark chocolate (grated)

AAAAAAAAAAAAAAAAAAAAAAAAAAAAAAAAAAAAAAAAAAAAAA

Instructions:

1. Preheat oven to 350 degrees F.

2. In a mixing bowl, place the cocoa powder and chocolate and cover with hot water. Whisk gently until powder and chocolate melt together to form a smooth, silky mixture. Refrigerate for 20 minutes, removing once to stir after 20 minutes has passed.

3. Sift together the sugar, flour, salt and baking soda, in a separate bowl. In a jug mix the eggs, oil, vanilla, and vinegar. Pour the oil mixture into the chilled chocolate mixture and mix will. Then add the wet ingredients to the dry ingredients, little by little, stirring continuously until well combined.

4. Fill each cupcake case with the mixture until 1/4 full and smooth the surface of each with the back of a spoon. Bake for approximately 18 to 20 minutes. Remove your cupcakes from the baking tin and place on a wire rack to cool.

5. Make a hole in each cupcake and fill with 1½ tablespoons of the desired filling.

6. To make the topping, whisk the heavy cream until you see it begins to form soft peaks. Add the sugar and whisk again, until stiff peaks start to form.

7. Swirl the cream onto the filled cupcakes and decorate with grated chocolate.

Recipe 5: White Chocolate and Pistachio Cupcakes

Totally sophisticated. These elegant cupcakes are guaranteed to impress your friends.

Yield: 12

Preparation Time: 1h 0mins

Total Cooking Time: 25mins

List of Ingredients:

Cupcakes:

- 1 ¼ cups white chocolate (chopped)
- 1 ½ cups all-purpose flour
- 1 teaspoon baking powder
- ½ teaspoons salt
- 1 cup full-fat milk
- 1 tablespoon vanilla
- ⅔ cup sugar
- 4 tablespoons butter (softened)
- 3 small eggs

Buttercream:

- 3 egg whites
- ¼ teaspoons cream of tartar
- ½ cup sugar
- ½ stick butter (softened)
- 1 cup confectioner's sugar
- ⅓ cup pistachios (ground to paste)
- Green food gel

Instructions:

1. Preheat oven to 350 degrees F.

2. Use a double boiler to melt the chocolate. Set aside.

3. In a bowl, sift together the baking powder, flour, and salt.

4. In a separate bowl, combine the vanilla and milk.

5. Using a stand mixer, cream the butter and sugar until fluffy and light. Mix in the eggs, and beat after each addition. Scrape down the bottom and sides of the bowl. Add in the chocolate and mix well.

12. Fold in the flour, little by little. Alternate each flour addition with splashes of the vanilla milk mixture, until both are used up. When the mixture is smooth and lump-free, fill each cupcake case with the mixture until 2/3 full and smooth the surface of each with the back of a spoon. Bake for approximately 28 minutes. Remove the cupcakes from the baking tin and place on a wire rack to cool.

6. To prepare the buttercream, use a stand mixer to whisk the eggs until they foam. Add cream of tartar and whisk until soft peaks are formed. Add the sugar and whisk again until stiff peaks are formed. The mixture should be glossy. Add the butter, a little at a time, then the confectioner's sugar. Add the pistachio paste and a few drops of green food gel. Beat on high speed for 2 minutes, until the buttercream is smooth and light.

7. Pipe the cooled cupcakes with the buttercream and decorate with crushed pistachios.

Recipe 6: Death by Chocolate Cupcakes

Melted dark chocolate and cocoa power make for a rich, fudgy sponge. Finished off with a decadent creamy frosting. This recipe is perfect for any true chocoholic.

Yield: 12

Preparation Time: 10mins

Total Cooking Time: 22mins

List of Ingredients:

Cupcakes:

- ¼ ounce unsalted butter
- ½ cup semisweet chocolate
- ½ cup cocoa powder (unsweetened)
- ½ teaspoons baking soda
- ¾ cup all-purpose flour
- ¾ teaspoons baking powder
- ¼ teaspoons salt
- ½ cup sugar
- ¼ cup brown sugar
- 3 small eggs (room temperature)
- 1 teaspoon vanilla extract
- ½ cup buttermilk

Frosting:

- ⅔ cup cocoa powder (unsweetened)
- 2¾ cup powdered sugar
- 6 tablespoons butter (unsalted and softened)
- 1 teaspoon vanilla extract
- 6 tablespoons heavy cream

AAA

Instructions:

1. Preheat oven to 350 degrees F.

2. In a microwave melt together butter and chocolate, stirring every 30 seconds. Set aside to cool.

3. In a mixing bowl, sift together cocoa powder, baking soda and powder, flour and salt. Add half the buttermilk.

4. In a separate bowl whisk together white and brown sugar, eggs, and vanilla. Pour the chocolate mixture and mix until velvety smooth.

5. Add the dry ingredients to the wet ingredients in 2 goes, stirring well after each addition. Combine the remaining buttermilk. Take care not to overmix; it is normal for your batter to be very thick.

6. Fill each cupcake case with the mixture until 2/3 full and smooth the surface of each with the back of a spoon. Bake for approximately 18 to 20 minutes. Remove the cupcakes from the baking tin and place on a wire rack to cool.

7. In the meantime, prepare the frosting. Combine the cocoa powder and powdered sugar and sift. Place to one side.

8. Use a handheld mixer to whisk up the butter until fluffy. Add the sugar/cocoa mix little by little, mixing continuously. Add a little salt if the mixture is excessively sweet.

9. Pipe the cooled cupcakes with the chocolate frosting and enjoy.

Recipe 7: S'more Cupcakes

Aptly named, as these cupcakes will leave you wanting s'more! This campfire staple makes a super tasty and messy treat!

Yield: 14

Preparation Time: 15mins

Total Cooking Time: 35mins

List of Ingredients:

Cupcakes:

- 1 cup plain flour
- 1 cup white sugar
- ¼ cup and ⅛ cup dark cocoa powder
- 1 teaspoon baking soda
- ½ teaspoons salt
- ½ cup buttermilk
- 1 medium egg
- ½ cup oil
- ½ cup water (boiling)
- ¾ teaspoons vanilla extract

Topping:

- 1 cup white sugar
- ½ teaspoons cream of tartar
- 4 egg whites
- Crackers (crumbed)

AAAAAAAAAAAAAAAAAAAAAAAAAAAAAAAAAAAAAAAAAAAAAA

Instructions:

1. Preheat oven to 330 degrees F.

2. Combine all dry ingredients in a mixing bowl. Add the buttermilk, egg, and oil and whisk.

3. In a jug mix water and vanilla extract and slowly pour it into the batter mix, continuously stirring.

4. Fill each of your cupcake case with the mixture until 2/3 full and smooth the surface of each with the back of a spoon. Bake for approximately 20 minutes. Remove the cupcakes out of the baking tin and then place on a wire rack to cool.

5. In the meantime, prepare the topping. In a metal bowl combine sugar, cream of tartar, and egg whites.

6. Place over simmering water and whisk mixture continuously until warm to touch and sugar dissolves. Take off the heat.

7. Use an electric mixer on low speed to whisk up the mixture until stiff peaks are formed; this should take approximately 6 minutes.

8. Spoon the marshmallow topping onto the cool cupcakes and sprinkle with crushed crackers.

Recipe 8: Jaffa Cupcakes

This classic combination of chocolate and orange has undergone a makeover. The addition of white chocolate gives these cupcakes a modern twist.

Yield: 8

Preparation Time: 15mins

Total Cooking Time: 20mins

List of Ingredients:

Cupcakes:

- 1 ¼ cups caster sugar
- 1 cup plain flour
- 1 teaspoon baking powder
- 1 ½ ounces unsalted butter
- 1 medium egg
- ½ cup milk
- ½ cup dark chocolate (melted and cooled)
- 3 tablespoons sugar
- Juice of 1 orange

Buttercream:

- 1 stick unsalted butter (softened)
- 3 tablespoons milk
- 2 ¼ cups powdered sugar
- Zest of 1 orange
- ¼ cup white chocolate (melted)

AAAAAAAAAAAAAAAAAAAAAAAAAAAAAAAAAAAAAAAAAAAAAA

Instructions:

1. Preheat oven 325 degrees F.

2. In a mixing bowl, sift together the sugar, flour, and baking powder. Add in the butter and mix until well combined.

3. In a separate jug, whisk together the egg, milk, and melted chocolate. Slowly pour the chocolate mixture into the mixing bowl, whisking continuously to combine all ingredients.

4. Fill each cupcake case with the mixture until 3/4 full and smooth the surface of each with the back of a spoon. Bake for approximately 18 to 20 minutes. Remove the cupcakes from the baking tin and place on a wire rack to cool.

5. In the meantime, mix sugar and orange juice in a jug. Slowly pour the mixture over the cupcakes while still warm and set aside to absorb and cool.

6. To make the buttercream, whip up the butter until fluffy and airy. Mix in the powdered sugar, little by little until well combined. Whisk in the milk, orange zest, and melted chocolate.

7. Pipe the cooled cupcakes with the chocolate buttercream and decorate with shavings of leftover chocolate.

Recipe 9: Salted Caramel and Chocolate Cupcakes

Melt in the mouth caramel is just calling out for a pinch of salt. Combine it with a moist chocolate sponge, and you have cupcake heaven.

Yield: 21

Preparation Time: 15mins

Total Cooking Time: 30mins

List of Ingredients:

Frosting:

- ¼ ounce salted butter
- ⅓ cup heavy cream
- 1 cup brown sugar
- 2½ cups confectioner's sugar (sifted)
- ¼ teaspoons salt
- 21 mini pretzels (for decoration)

Cupcakes:

- 1 box devil's food cake mix
- 5 small eggs
- 1 box of instant chocolate pudding mix
- ½ cup vegetable oil
- 1 cup Greek yogurt
- ½ cup milk

AAAAAAAAAAAAAAAAAAAAAAAAAAAAAAAAAAAAAAAAAAAAAAAA

Instructions:

1. Preheat oven to 350 degrees F.

2. First, prepare the frosting. In a saucepan over low heat, melt butter, cream and brown sugar, until sugar dissolves. Bring to a 'bubble' and leave for 2 minutes. Take off the heat and set to one side. Mix in the confectioner's sugar little by little. Add salt.

3. To make the batter, use an electric whisk to mix the pudding and cake mix, oil, eggs, yogurt, and milk.

4. Fill each cupcake case with the mixture until 2/3 full and smooth the surface of each with the back of a spoon. Bake for approximately 25 minutes. Remove the cupcakes from the baking tin and place on a wire rack to cool.

5. Frost the cooled cupcakes with the frosting and drizzle with leftover caramel.

Recipe 10: Mint Chocolate Cupcakes

Everyone's favorite ice cream flavor presented as a tasty bite-sized cupcake. Dark chocolate and refreshing peppermint flavors make this recipe light but still indulgent.

Yield: 12

Preparation Time: 30mins

Total Cooking Time: 25mins

List of Ingredients:

Cupcakes:

- 1 ¼ cups muscovado sugar
- 1 ½ cups unsalted butter (softened)
- 3 medium eggs (beaten)
- 1 cup self-raising flour (sifted)
- 1/8 cup cocoa powder (sifted)
- ¾ teaspoons baking soda
- ¾ teaspoons baking powder
- ½ teaspoons salt
- 1 cup dark chocolate chips

Icing:

- ½ stick unsalted butter (softened)
- 2 cups powdered sugar
- 2 teaspoons water
- ¼ teaspoons mint extract
- ¼ teaspoons green food coloring
- 12 after dinner mints

AAAAAAAAAAAAAAAAAAAAAAAAAAAAAAAAAAAAAAAAAAAAAAA

Instructions:

1. Preheat the oven to 360 degrees F.

2. Using a large mixing bowl combine the butter and sugar. Add the eggs slowly, mixing continuously. Add the flour, cocoa powder, baking soda, salt and baking powder.

3. Use a metal spoon to fold in the dry ingredients and add chocolate chips.

4. Fill each cupcake case with the mixture until 3/4 full and smooth the surface of each with the back of a spoon. Bake 25 minutes, or until a cocktail stick inserted into the center comes out totally clean. Remove the cupcakes from the baking tin and place on a wire rack and leave to cool.

5. Prepare the icing. Whisk together butter and powdered sugar with 2 teaspoons of boiling water. Add the mint extract and color with food dye until the icing is peppermint colored.

6. Pipe the cooled cupcakes with the icing and decorate with an after-dinner mint.

Chapter II - Fruit Cupcakes

AAAAAAAAAAAAAAAAAAAAAAAAAAAAAAAAAAAAAAAAAAAAAA

Recipe 11: Watermelon Cupcakes

Easy and fun to make, kids especially will enjoy baking these super cute, colorful cupcakes. They're almost too pretty to eat!

Yield: 12

Preparation Time: 15mins

Total Cooking Time: 10mins

List of Ingredients:

- ⅔ cup sugar
- 6 tablespoons unsalted butter (softened)
- ½ cup sour cream
- 3 medium egg whites
- 1½ teaspoons baking powder
- ¼ teaspoons salt
- 1 cup and 2 tablespoons all-purpose flour
- 1 teaspoon vanilla extract
- Bright green food coloring

Buttercream:

- ½ cup vegetable shortening
- ½ ounce unsalted butter (room temperature)
- 3½ cups confectioner's sugar
- ¾ teaspoons watermelon Kool-Aid powder
- Red food coloring
- Chocolate chips

AAAAAAAAAAAAAAAAAAAAAAAAAAAAAAAAAAAAAAAAAAAAAAAA

Instructions:

1. Preheat oven to 375 degrees F.

2. Cream the sugar and butter together in a large mixing bowl. Fold in the sour cream. Beat in the egg whites.

3. Using a spatula, mix in the vanilla and sour cream.

4. In a separate bowl, sift the flour, baking powder, and salt, and combine.

5. Add the dry to the wet ingredients by a little at a time. Mix gently and don't forget to scrape the whole of the mixing bowl. Use several drops of coloring to make a bright green batter.

6. Fill each cupcake case with the mixture until 1/2 full and smooth the surface of each with the back of a spoon. Bake for approximately 10 minutes. Remove the cupcakes from the baking tin and place on a wire rack to cool.

7. In the meantime, prepare the buttercream. Use an electric mixer to beat together the vegetable shortening and butter, for 2 minutes.

8. Use a spatula to mix in 2 cups of confectioner's sugar. Switch to using an electric mixer and slowly add the remaining sugar until your buttercream reaches the desired pipeable consistency.

9. Mix in the Kool-Aid and use a few drops of coloring to make the buttercream watermelon pink.

10. To assemble, pipe the green cupcakes with the pink buttercream. Decorate with chocolate chips to resemble watermelon seeds.

Recipe 12: Banoffee Pie Cupcakes

Decadent Dulce de Leche buttercream sitting atop a moist banana sponge is every banoffee lover's dream. It's a classic pairing for a reason.

Yield: 12

Preparation Time: 15mins

Total Cooking Time: 20mins

List of Ingredients:

Cupcakes:

- 2 medium eggs
- 1 cup unrefined golden caster sugar
- 1 cup unsalted butter (softened)
- 1 teaspoon baking powder
- 1 ½ cups self-raising flour
- 3 overripe bananas (mashed)
- ¼ cup fudge pieces

Buttercream:

- 1 ½ cups unrefined icing sugar
- ¾ stick unsalted butter
- ¼ cup Dulce de Leche

AAAAAAAAAAAAAAAAAAAAAAAAAAAAAAAAAAAAAAAAAAAAAAAA

Instructions:

1. Preheat oven to 350 degrees F.

2. In a large mixing bowl, crack the eggs, then add the sugar and butter. Use an electric mixer to whisk together for approximately 5 minutes, until fluffy and light.

3. Sieve the baking powder and flour into the bowl, a little at a time, continuously mixing. Add the banana and fudge and fold gently, until well combined.

4. Fill each cupcake case with the mixture until 2/3 full and smooth the surface of each with the back of a spoon. Bake for approximately 15 to 20 minutes, until they are golden brown and spring to the touch. Remove the cupcakes from the baking tin and place on a wire rack to cool.

5. In the meantime, beat together the icing sugar and butter until you achieve a smooth texture. Add one tablespoon of Dulce de Leche and fold in.

6. Take the cooled cupcakes and pipe with buttercream. Drizzle with the remaining Dulce de Leche.

Recipe 13: Very Berry Cupcakes

Packed with forest fruits, these very berry cupcakes are bursting with fruit flavor. Topped with a colorful berry frosting, these would brighten any party spread.

Yield: 20

Preparation Time: 15mins

Total Cooking Time: 25-30mins

List of Ingredients:

Cupcakes:

- 3 teaspoons baking powder
- ½ teaspoons salt
- 2 ½ cups caster sugar
- 11 ¼ cups all-purpose flour
- 1 stick unsalted butter (softened)
- 2 medium eggs
- 1½ cups milk
- ½ cup vegetable oil
- 2 tablespoons Greek yogurt
- 1 teaspoon vanilla extract
- 2 cups frozen mixed berries

Frosting:

- ½ cup butter (softened)
- 2 cups cream cheese
- 4 cups confectioner's sugar
- 2 teaspoons berry jam
- 2 drops purple food gel

AAAAAAAAAAAAAAAAAAAAAAAAAAAAAAAAAAAAAAAAAAAAAAAA

Instructions:

1. Preheat oven to 360 degrees F.

2. Use a standing mixer to combine the baking powder, salt, caster sugar, and flour. Add in the butter and mix until the texture resembles fine sand.

3. Whisk the eggs, milk, oil, yogurt, and vanilla in a separate bowl.

4. Slowly pour the wet ingredients into the dry ingredients, stirring continuously for 40 seconds. Fold in the frozen berries. Midway, scrape down the sides of the bowl.

5. Fill each cupcake case with the mixture until 3/4 full and smooth the surface of each with the back of a spoon. Bake for approximately 25 minutes, possibly longer. Remove the cupcakes from the baking tin and place on a wire rack to cool.

6. In the meantime, prepare the cream cheese frosting. Mix the butter and cream cheese. Add in the sugar and continue to mix until smooth and creamy. Mix in the jam and gel coloring, whisking quickly to prevent the mix becoming too runny.

7. Pipe the cool cupcakes with the cream cheese frosting and enjoy!

Recipe 14: Blueberry 'Muffin' Cupcakes

A sweet twist on the original blueberry muffin. Fresh blueberries are mixed into the cupcake batter and topped with blueberry cream cheese frosting.

Yield: 12

Preparation Time: 25mins

Total Cooking Time: 20mins

List of Ingredients:

Cupcakes:

- ¼ teaspoons baking powder
- ½ teaspoons baking soda
- ½ teaspoons salt
- 1⅔ cups all-purpose flour
- 1 stick unsalted butter (softened)
- ⅔ cup granulated sugar
- 2 medium eggs
- 1 teaspoon vanilla extract
- ¾ cup sour cream
- 1¼ fresh blueberries

Icing:

- 1 cup full-fat cream cheese (room temperature
- ⅓ pound unsalted butter (softened)
- 2⅔ cups confectioner's sugar (sifted)
- ½ teaspoons vanilla extract
- ¼ cup blueberry jam (strained)

Instructions:

1. Preheat oven to 375 degrees F.

2. Sift together the baking powder, baking soda, salt, and flour.

3. In a separate bowl, use an electric mixer on a medium speed to beat together butter and sugar. When the mix is light and very fluffy, whisk in the eggs, one at a time. Keep scraping down the sides of the bowl. Add in the extract of vanilla. Reduce the mixer speed to low and whisk in the flour and sour cream, little by little.

4. Gently fold in the fresh blueberries.

5. Fill each cupcake case with the mixture until 2/3 full and smooth the surface of each with the back of a spoon. Bake for just over 20 minutes, until golden brown. To test if ready, pierce the center with a cocktail stick. If moist crumbs are attached to the cocktail stick when removed, the cupcakes are ready. Remove the cupcakes from the baking tin and place on a wire rack to cool.

6. Meanwhile, make the buttercream. Using a mixer on medium speed, whisk together the cream cheese and butter for approximately 2 to 3 minutes. Reduce whisk speed to low and slowly add in confectioner's sugar and vanilla. Beat for 2 minutes until mixture is fluffy, light and well combined. Pour the jam directly on top of the icing mixture in the bowl and do not stir.

7. Transfer the icing to a pastry bag and pipe each of the cooled cupcakes. Serve immediately.

Recipe 15: Strawberries and Cream Cupcakes

This classic British flavor pairing of strawberries and cream is the nation's favorite for a reason! Enjoy with a cup of afternoon tea for a truly British experience.

Yield: 22

Preparation Time: 10mins

Total Cooking Time: 15mins

List of Ingredients:

Cupcakes:

- 1¼ cups water
- 4 cups instant white cake mix
- 3 egg whites
- 1 teaspoon almond extract
- 2 teaspoons vanilla extract
- 3 tablespoons unsalted butter (melted)

Filling:

- 1 cup whipping cream
- ¼ cup confectioner's sugar
- 1 teaspoon vanilla extract
- 2½ cups fresh sweet strawberries (sliced)

AAAAAAAAAAAAAAAAAAAAAAAAAAAAAAAAAAAAAAAAAAAAAAAA

Instructions:

1. Preheat oven to 350 degrees F.

2. In a bowl, combine the water, cake mix, egg whites, almond and vanilla extracts, and butter.

3. Fill each cupcake case with the mixture until 3/4 full and smooth the surface of each with the back of a spoon. Bake for approximately 15 minutes. Remove the cupcakes from the baking tin and place on a wire rack to cool.

4. To make the filling, use an electric whisk to whip up the heavy cream, powdered sugar and vanilla extract. The mixture is ready when stiff peaks begin to form. Fold the strawberries into the filling.

5. Slice the top off each cupcake and set aside. Spoon the strawberry/cream mixture onto each cupcake and then top with the sponge 'lid'. Decorate with a dusting of confectioner's sugar and serve.

Recipe 16: Coconut Lime Cupcakes

These coconut and lime cupcakes will have you dreaming of the Caribbean. Sweet coconut and zingy lime make the perfect indulgent, yet refreshing, treat.

Yield: 16

Preparation Time: 15mins

Total Cooking Time: 15mins

List of Ingredients:

Cupcakes:

- ½ teaspoons baking soda
- 1 teaspoon baking powder
- ½ teaspoons salt
- 1¼ cups flour
- ¾ cup sugar
- 2 medium eggs
- 1 teaspoon coconut extract
- ¾ cup canned coconut cream
- ½ cup olive oil
- 3 teaspoons lime zest
- 4 tablespoons fresh lime juice

Icing:

- 2 cups full fat cream cheese
- ½ cup unsalted butter (softened)
- 1½ cups powdered sugar
- 1½ teaspoons coconut extract (for frosting)
- 3 tablespoons sweetened flaked coconut (toasted)
- Slices of lime (quartered)

AA

Instructions:

1. Preheat oven to 400 degrees F.

2. In a large mixing bowl, whisk together the baking soda, baking powder, salt, and flour.

3. In a separate bowl mix the sugar and eggs until smooth. Add in the coconut extract and cream, olive oil, and lime zest and juice.

4. Fold the dry ingredients into the wet ingredients taking care not to over-mix.

5. Fill each cupcake case with the mixture until 2/3 full and smooth the surface of each with the back of a spoon. Bake for 13 to 15 minutes, until the sponge springs back on light pressing. Remove the cupcakes from the baking tin and place on a wire rack to cool.

6. Meanwhile, prepare the frosting. Using a hand mixer on medium speed, beat together the cream cheese and butter. Add the powdered sugar and coconut extract together and whisk until just combined.

7. Transfer the frosting to a pastry bag and pipe the cool cupcakes.

8. Decorate with toasted coconut and a slice of lime.

Recipe 17: Raspberry and White Chocolate Cupcakes

Tart, fresh raspberries nestle on top of a creamy white chocolate ganache frosting, creating a perfect balance of flavors. Simple but refined.

Yield: 14

Preparation Time: 2h 35mins

Total Cooking Time: 25mins

List of Ingredients:

Cupcakes:

- ¾ cup caster sugar
- 1 ½ cups butter (room temperature)
- 2 medium eggs
- 1 ¼ cups white chocolate (melted and cooled)
- 1/3 cup whole milk
- 1 cup self-raising flour
- 1 cup plain flour
- 1 ¼ cup fresh raspberries

Frosting:

- 2 cups white chocolate (finely chopped)
- 1/3 cup thick cream
- 1 stick butter (chopped)

AAAAAAAAAAAAAAAAAAAAAAAAAAAAAAAAAAAAAAAAAAAAAAAA

Instructions:

1. Preheat oven to 360 degrees F.

2. Beat together the sugar and butter with an electric whisk. Add one egg and beat, then add the second egg and beat again. Mix in the melted chocolate and milk.

3. In a separate bowl, combine all of the dry ingredients and then add them into the wet ingredients, little by little, until only just combined.

8. Fill each cupcake case with the mixture until 3/4 full and smooth the surface of each with the back of a spoon. Bake for approximately 25 minutes. Remove the cupcakes from the baking tin and place on a wire rack to cool.

4. In the meantime, prepare the frosting. Melt the chocolate and cream in a microwave, removing every minute to stir. When the mixture is velvety and smooth, add in the butter. Stir until well combined. Refrigerate until the mixture is firm and can be easily spread, approximately 2 hours.

5. Beat the chilled frosting with an electric whisk until it's creamy and smooth. Transfer to a piping bag and swirl on each of the cupcakes. Decorate each cupcake with a couple of fresh raspberries.

Recipe 18: Lemon Meringue Pie Cupcakes

Tart lemon curd filling, sweetened by a fluffy white meringue topping make these a delicious bittersweet delight. A very classy cupcake indeed.

Yield: 12

Preparation Time: 1h

Total Cooking Time: 25-30mins

List of Ingredients:

Cupcakes:

- 1 stick unsalted butter (softened)
- ¾ cup white sugar
- 2 teaspoons vanilla extract
- 2 medium eggs (room temperature)
- 1½ teaspoons baking powder
- 1½ cups plain flour
- 1 teaspoon salt
- ½ cup buttermilk

Curd:

- 1½ tablespoons lemon zest
- ½ cup fresh lemon juice
- ½ cup white sugar
- 3 medium egg yolks
- 6 tablespoons butter
- Meringue:
- 3 medium egg whites
- 1 teaspoon almond extract
- ½ cup sugar

AA

Instructions:

1. Preheat the oven to 350 degrees F.

2. Cream butter and sugar together in a large bowl. When light and fluffy add the vanilla extract and eggs, whisk until well combined.

3. Combine the baking powder, flour, and salt in a separate mixing bowl. Slowly incorporate the buttermilk, pouring it in little by little and taking care not to overmix.

4. Fill each cupcake case with the mixture until 2/3 full and smooth the surface of each with the back of a spoon. Bake for 25 to 30 mins, or until a cocktail stick inserted into the center comes out clean. Remove the cupcakes from the baking tin and place on a rack to cool.

5. Prepare the lemon curd. Using a double boiler, whisk together the lemon zest and juice, sugar and egg yolks, over a medium to high heat for approximately 7 minutes. The curd is ready when it is thick and able to coat the back of your spoon. Take off the heat and immediately mix in the butter until your curd is super glossy and smooth.

6. Strain the lemon curd ensuring no lumps remain. Cover and refrigerate until needed for assembly.

7. Cut a conical hole in the center of each cupcake using a small knife. Scoop out a little of the sponge and fill the space with curd.

8. To prepare the meringue, use a standing mixer to whisk the egg whites for 2 to 3 minutes until you achieve stiff peaks. Add in the vanilla extract and sugar and whisk again to combine.

9. Spoon the meringue carefully onto each cupcake. Place the topped cupcakes back into the oven and broil for 3 to 4 minutes on a high heat.

10. Remove from oven and allow to cool a little before enjoying!

Recipe 19: Passionfruit Cheesecake Cupcakes

This popular summer dessert has been transformed into a delicious fruity cupcake. Punchy passionfruit drizzles and swirls of tangy cream cheese frosting are sure to satisfy any cheesecake lover.

Yield: 24

Preparation Time: 20mins

Total Cooking Time: 25mins

List of Ingredients:

Cupcakes:

- 3 teaspoons baking powder
- 2/3 teaspoons salt
- 9½ ounces caster sugar
- 1 ¾ cups all-purpose flour
- 1 cup unsalted butter (softened)
- 2 large eggs
- 1½ cups milk
- 2 tablespoons Greek yogurt
- 1 teaspoon vanilla extract
- ½ cup vegetable oil
- 1 ¼ cups fresh passionfruit

Frosting:

- ½ cup butter (softened)
- 2 cups cream cheese
- 4 cups confectioner's sugar
- 2 teaspoons vanilla extract

AAAAAAAAAAAAAAAAAAAAAAAAAAAAAAAAAAAAAAAAAAAAAAAA

Instructions:

1. Preheat oven to 360 degrees F.

2. Use a stand mixer on a low speed to blend the baking powder, salt, caster sugar, and flour. Add in the butter and continue to mix until the texture is similar to fine sand.

3. In a separate bowl, add the eggs, milk, yogurt, vanilla, and oil and whisk together well.

4. Slowly pour the wet ingredients into the dry ingredients and mix for 30 to 40 seconds, stopping midway to scrape down the sides of the mixing bowl.

5. Fill each cupcake case with the mixture until 3/4 full and smooth the surface of each with the back of a spoon. Spoon a little passionfruit onto the top of each cupcake and swirl into the batter with a cocktail stick. Bake for approximately 20 to 25 minutes. Remove the cupcakes from the baking tin and place on a wire rack to cool.

6. In the meantime, prepare the cream cheese frosting. Mix the butter and cream cheese. Add in the sugar and powdered vanilla and continue to mix until smooth and creamy.

7. Pipe the cooled cupcakes with the frosting and drizzle with a little more passionfruit.

Recipe 20: Mango and Vanilla Cupcakes

Bursting with flavor, these truly tropical cupcakes are a pleasure to eat. Exotic mango, smooth vanilla and a hint of coconut, could it get any better!?

Yield: 12

Preparation Time: 15mins

Total Cooking Time: 20mins

List of Ingredients:

Cupcakes:

- ½ teaspoons baking powder
- ¼ teaspoons baking soda
- ¼ teaspoons salt
- 1½ cups all-purpose flour
- ½ cup unsalted butter (melted, cooled)
- 1 cup white sugar
- 1 teaspoon vanilla extract
- ¾ cup whole milk
- ¼ cup coconut yogurt
- 2 small eggs

Buttercream:

- ¾ cup unsalted butter (room temperature)
- ¼ teaspoons salt
- ½ teaspoons vanilla extract
- ½ cup pureed mango
- 4 cups icing sugar

AAAAAAAAAAAAAAAAAAAAAAAAAAAAAAAAAAAAAAAAAA

Instructions:

1. Preheat oven to 350 degrees F.

2. In a mixing bowl, combine the baking powder and soda, salt, and flour.

3. In another bowl, cream the butter and sugar. Mix in the vanilla, milk, yogurt, and eggs. Add in the dry ingredients and whisk until smooth, taking care not to overmix.

4. Fill each cupcake case with the mixture until 3/4 full and smooth the surface of each with the back of a spoon. Bake for approximately 20 minutes. Remove the cupcakes from the baking tin and place on a wire rack to cool.

5. In the meantime, prepare the buttercream. Whip up the butter, then add the salt, vanilla, and pureed mango. Add in the icing sugar, a little at a time, and continue to stir together until just combined.

6. Pipe the cooled cupcakes with the buttercream and serve.

Chapter III - Vegan/Gluten Free Cupcakes

AAAAAAAAAAAAAAAAAAAAAAAAAAAAAAAAAAAAAAAAAAAAA

Recipe 21: Vegan Vanilla Cupcakes

A classic vanilla cupcake that literally anyone can enjoy. Not only vegan, but these cupcakes are also gluten, dairy, and egg free. All the more reason to go back for second helpings.

Yield: 12

Preparation Time: 15mins

Total Cooking Time: 20mins

List of Ingredients:

Cupcakes:

- 1¾ cups gluten-free flour
- 1 teaspoon baking powder
- ½ teaspoons baking soda
- ½ teaspoons salt
- ½ cup vanilla coconut milk (unsweetened)
- ½ cup water
- 1 tablespoon white vinegar
- 1 cup granulated sugar
- ⅓ cup canola oil
- 1 tablespoon organic vanilla extract

Buttercream:

- ½ cup vegan butter (cold)
- ¼ cup non-hydrogenated shortening
- 3 cups confectioner's sugar (sifted)
- 3 tablespoons coconut milk creamer
- 1 teaspoon organic vanilla extract

AAAAAAAAAAAAAAAAAAAAAAAAAAAAAAAAAAAAAAAAAAAAAA

Instructions:

1. Preheat oven to 350 degrees F.

2. Sift together the dry ingredients and place to one side.

3. In a separate bowl, combine the wet ingredients and allow to sit for 2 minutes.

4. Add the dry ingredients to the wet, little by little, mixing continuously until just combined.

5. Fill each cupcake case with the mixture until 2/3 full and smooth the surface of each with the back of a spoon. Bake for approximately 20 minutes. Remove the cupcakes from the baking tin and place on a wire rack to cool.

6. In the meantime, prepare the buttercream. Beat the butter and shortening using and electric whisk. Add the remaining ingredients, a little at a time, beating between each addition.

7. Pipe the cooled cupcakes with the buttercream.

Recipe 22: Carrot and Vanilla Cupcakes

These carrot cake cupcakes are so light and moist; you would never guess they were vegan-friendly. A sweet vanilla frosting compliments the spiced sponge perfectly.

Yield: 24

Preparation Time: 6h

Total Cooking Time: 25mins

List of Ingredients:

Cupcakes:

- 3 cups of all-purpose flour
- 1 tablespoon baking powder
- 1 tablespoon baking soda
- 1 teaspoon xanthan gum
- 1½ teaspoons sea salt
- 1 tablespoon cinnamon
- 2 teaspoons ginger
- ½ teaspoons nutmeg
- ⅔ cup coconut oil
- 1 cup agave nectar
- 1 cup rice milk
- 1 tablespoon vanilla
- ½ cup water (hot)
- 3 cups carrot (finely grated)

Frosting:

- 1½ cups soy milk (unsweetened)
- ¾ cup soy milk powder
- ¼ cup agave nectar
- 1 tablespoon coconut flour
- 1 tablespoon vanilla
- 2 tablespoons fresh squeezed lemon juice
- 1½ coconut oil

AAAAAAAAAAAAAAAAAAAAAAAAAAAAAAAAAAAAAAAAAAAAAAA

Instructions:

1. Preheat oven to 325 degrees F.

2. Start by preparing the frosting. Mix the soy milk and powder, agave nectar, coconut flour, and vanilla, for 2 minutes.

3. Add the lemon juice and oil, mix until well incorporated. Refrigerate for 5 to 6 hours, until firm for piping.

4. To make the batter, use a food processor to combine the dry ingredients.

5. Add in the wet ingredients.

6. Slowly pour in hot water, until the batter becomes smooth.

7. Fold the carrots into the batter until evenly distributed.

8. Fill each cupcake case with the mixture until 2/3 full and smooth the surface of each with the back of a spoon. Bake for approximately 24 to 26 minutes. Remove the cupcakes from the baking tin and place on a wire rack to cool.

9. Spread a thick layer of frosting neatly on each cooled cupcake.

Recipe 23: Strawberry Beet Cupcakes

Fresh strawberries are included in the sponge to make a super moist cupcake. Piped with naturally pink frosting, these healthy treats will appeal to kids too!

Yield: 12

Preparation Time: 15mins

Total Cooking Time: 30mins

List of Ingredients:

Cupcakes:

- 1 teaspoon white vinegar
- 1 cup coconut milk
- ¼ cup melted coconut oil
- ½ cup granulated sugar
- ¼ cup pureed beetroot
- 2 teaspoons organic vanilla extract
- 1½ cups all-purpose flour
- ½ teaspoons baking powder
- ¾ teaspoons baking soda
- ¼ teaspoons salt
- ½ cup strawberries (chopped)

Frosting:

- ¼ ounce vegan butter
- 2½ cups confectioner's sugar
- 1 tablespoon pureed beetroot
- ½ teaspoons organic vanilla extract
- Splash of coconut milk

AAAAAAAAAAAAAAAAAAAAAAAAAAAAAAAAAAAAAAAAAAAAAAAA

Instructions:

1. Preheat the oven to 350 degrees F.

2. Whisk the vinegar and milk together and set aside for 2 minutes.

3. Add in the oil, sugar, and vanilla. Whisk until the mixture foams. Add the beetroot and whisk again.

4. Sift the dry ingredients into the wet and mix well, until there are no remaining lumps.

5. Fold in the strawberries until evenly distributed.

6. Fill each cupcake case with the mixture until 2/3 full and smooth the surface of each with the back of a spoon. Bake for approximately 30 minutes. Remove the cupcakes from the baking tin and place on a wire rack to cool.

7. In the meantime, prepare the frosting.

8. Cream the butter using and electric whisk. Add in the confectioner's sugar, a little at a time. Mix in the beetroot and vanilla. Add the milk in very small amount, until the desired consistency is achieved.

9. Frost the cooled cupcakes with the frosting.

Recipe 24: Chocolate Cupcakes

A guilt-free way to satisfy your chocolate cravings. Bake and enjoy slathered in lashings of fluffy chocolate frosting.

Yield: 14

Preparation Time: 20mins

Total Cooking Time: 20mins

List of Ingredients:

Cupcakes:

- 1¼ cups gluten free flour
- ½ cup organic cocoa powder
- 1 teaspoon baking powder
- 1 teaspoon baking soda
- ½ teaspoons salt
- ½ cup water (cold)
- ½ cup coconut milk (unsweetened)
- 1 tablespoon white vinegar
- ⅓ cup sunflower oil
- ½ cup sugar
- 1½ teaspoons organic vanilla extract

Frosting:

- 3 tablespoons organic shortening
- ½ cup vegan butter (room temperature)
- ¾ cup organic cocoa powder
- 2¾ cups confectioner's sugar
- 1 teaspoon organic vanilla extract
- 5 tablespoons coconut milk coffee creamer

Instructions:

1. Preheat oven to 350 degrees F.

2. Sift the dry ingredients together in a large bowl.

3. In a separate bowl, mix the water, vinegar and coconut milk and set aside for 1 minute. Add the oil, sugar, and vanilla.

4. Add the flour to the wet mix, little by little. Whisk together until all ingredients are well combined, and the batter is smooth and lump-free.

5. Fill each cupcake case with the mixture until 3/4 full and smooth the surface of each with the back of a spoon. Bake for just under 20 minutes. Remove the cupcakes from the baking tin and place on a wire rack to cool.

6. In the meantime, prepare the frosting. Use a stand mixer to beat together the shortening, butter, cocoa powder, confectioner's sugar, vanilla, and coffee creamer for 2 minutes.

7. Take the cooled cupcakes and pipe with chocolate frosting.

Recipe 25: Snickerdoodle Cupcakes

Cinnamon spiced sponge and buttery vegan frosting. These scrumptious cupcakes are best enjoyed while curled up in front of a crackling fire.

Yield: 12

Preparation Time: 10mins

Total Cooking Time: 25mins

List of Ingredients:

Cupcakes:

- 1½ cups all-purpose flour
- ¾ cups brown sugar
- ¼ cup granulated sugar
- ½ teaspoons baking soda
- ½ teaspoons salt
- ¼ teaspoons ground cinnamon
- ¾ cup water (cold)
- ½ cup canola oil
- 2½ teaspoons organic vanilla extract
- 1 teaspoon white vinegar

Frosting:

- ¼ cup vegan butter
- 2¾ cups powdered sugar
- ¾ teaspoons ground cinnamon
- 3 tablespoons almond milk
- Cinnamon for decoration

AAAAAAAAAAAAAAAAAAAAAAAAAAAAAAAAAAAAAAAAAAAAAA

Instructions:

1. Preheat oven to 375 degrees F.

2. Sift dry ingredients together in a bowl. Add in the wet ingredients and whisk until smooth and no lumps remain.

3. Fill each cupcake case with the mixture until 2/3 full and smooth the surface of each with the back of a spoon. Bake for 21 to 23 minutes. Remove the cupcakes from the baking tin and place on a wire rack to cool.

4. In the meantime, prepare the frosting. Whip the butter with an electric whisk. Add the confectioner's sugar, little by little and continue to whisk. Mix in the milk a tablespoon at a time, until the frosting reaches the desired consistency.

5. Spread a generous layer of frosting onto each cooled cupcake and decorate with a dusting of ground cinnamon.

Recipe 26: Chocolate Chip Cupcakes

These chocolate chip cupcakes are frosted with a vegan marshmallow fluff. Made from only 3 ingredients, this frosting is a game changer.

Yield: 14

Preparation Time: 30mins

Total Cooking Time: 20mins

List of Ingredients:

Cupcakes:

- 1½ cups gluten free flour
- ½ teaspoons baking soda
- ½ teaspoons salt
- 1 cup sugar substitute
- ½ teaspoons xanthan gum
- ½ cup veganaise
- 1 teaspoon organic vanilla extract
- 2 tablespoons water (cold)

Marshmallow Fluff:

- Water drained from one can of chickpeas
- ⅓ cup xylitol
- 1 teaspoon organic vanilla extract

AAAAAAAAAAAAAAAAAAAAAAAAAAAAAAAAAAAAAAAAAAA

Instructions:

1. Preheat oven to 350 degrees F.

2. In a mixing bowl, sift together the dry ingredients.

3. Whisk together the remaining ingredients, in a separate bowl.

4. Add all the dry ingredients to the wet, little by little and mix until just combined.

5. Fill each cupcake case with the mixture until 1/2 full and smooth the surface of each with the back of a spoon. Bake for just under 20 minutes. Remove the cupcakes from the baking tin and place on a wire rack to completly cool.

6. In the meantime, prepare the marshmallow fluff. Use a stand mixer to whip up all ingredients. Beat for approximately 15 minutes, until stiff peaks form.

7. Spread a thick layer of fluff over each cooled cupcake.

Recipe 27: Peach and Honey Buttercream Cupcakes

Peaches and honey go together like cupcakes and frosting. For best results, make with fresh, in-season peaches for a more intense, fruity flavor.

Yield: 12

Preparation Time: 15mins

Total Cooking Time: 45mins

List of Ingredients:

Cupcakes:

- 1 teaspoon apple cider vinegar
- 1 cup vanilla soy milk
- ⅓ cup oil
- 2 teaspoons organic vanilla extract
- ¾ cup sugar
- 2 large peaches (pitted, peeled and pureed)
- 1¼ cup all-purpose flour
- ¾ teaspoons baking soda
- ½ teaspoons baking powder
- Pinch of salt

Buttercream:

- 4 tablespoons vegan honey
- ¼ ounce vegan butter (softened)
- 1¾ cups confectioner's sugar
- 1 tablespoon sweetened almond milk

AAAAAAAAAAAAAAAAAAAAAAAAAAAAAAAAAAAAAAAAAAAAAAAA

Instructions:

1. Preheat oven to 350 degrees F.

2. In a large bowl, whisk vinegar and milk and set to one side for 2 minutes.

3. Add the oil, sugar, and vanilla and whisk until it foams. Stir in the peaches.

4. Sift the dry ingredients over the wet ingredients and stir until just combined with no lumps remaining.

5. Fill each cupcake case with the mixture until 3/4 full and smooth the surface of each with the back of a spoon. Bake for just over 28 minutes. Remove the cupcakes from the baking tin and place on a wire rack to cool.

6. In the meantime, prepare the buttercream. Cream the 'honey' and butter together in a large bowl.

7. Using an electric whisk, mix the confectioner's sugar, a little at a time.

8. Pour in the almond milk slowly, whisking continuously.

9. Pipe the cooled cupcakes with the honey buttercream.

Recipe 28: Funfetti Cupcakes

Dairy, egg, and gluten free but you'd never know it! A great healthy alternative for any party or celebration.

Yield: 10

Preparation Time: 10mins

Total Cooking Time: 15mins

List of Ingredients:

Cupcakes:

- 1½ cups gluten free flour
- ¾ cup sugar
- 1½ teaspoons baking powder
- ½ teaspoons baking soda
- ½ teaspoons xanthan gum
- ¼ teaspoons salt
- ¾ cup almond milk
- 2 teaspoons apple cider vinegar
- ⅓ cup oil
- 2 tablespoons vegan sprinkles

Frosting:

- ⅓ cup vegan butter
- ⅓ cup non-hydrogenated shortening
- 2½ cups confectioner's sugar
- 1 tablespoon almond milk
- 1 teaspoon organic vanilla extract
- Vegan sprinkles

AAAAAAAAAAAAAAAAAAAAAAAAAAAAAAAAAAAAAAAAAAA

Instructions:

1. Preheat oven to 350 degrees F.

2. Sift together all dry ingredients.

3. In a separate bowl, whisk together all wet ingredients (excluding sprinkles).

4. Add the dry ingredients to the wet, little by little, mixing with a wooden spoon. Add in the sprinkles.

5. Fill each cupcake case with the mixture until 2/3 full and smooth the surface of each with the back of a spoon. Bake for just less than 20 minutes. Remove the cupcakes from the baking tin and place on a wire rack to cool.

6. In the meantime, prepare the frosting. Use an electric whisk to cream the butter and shortening. Add the confectioner's sugar a little at a time.

7. Add in the milk and vanilla. Whisk until the frosting is fluffy but firm.

8. Spread a generous layer of frosting over each cooled cupcake and decorate with sprinkles.

Recipe 29: Natural Red Velvet Cupcakes

A healthier alternative to the classic red velvet. Beet juice is a great natural alternative to artificial food coloring and gives these cupcakes their trademark red color.

Yield: 12

Preparation Time: 10mins

Total Cooking Time: 15mins

List of Ingredients:

Cupcake:

- 1 cup all-purpose flour
- 6 tablespoons organic cocoa powder (unsweetened)
- ½ teaspoons salt
- ½ teaspoons baking soda
- 1 cup xylitol
- ½ cup chocolate chips
- ½ cup veganaise
- 3 teaspoons organic vanilla extract
- ½ cup beetroot juice
- 4 tablespoons water

Frosting:

- ½ cup vegan cream cheese
- 1 teaspoon organic vanilla extract
- 8 tablespoons confectioner's sugar
- ½ cup silken tofu
- 4 tablespoons almond milk

AAAAAAAAAAAAAAAAAAAAAAAAAAAAAAAAAAAAAAAAAAAAAAA

Instructions:

1. Preheat oven to 350 degrees F.

2. Sift all dry ingredients into a bowl and combine.

3. In a separate bowl, whisk together all the wet ingredients, until the mix is smooth.

4. Add the dry ingredients to the wet, little by little. Mix until just combined.

5. Fill each cupcake case with the mixture until 3/4 full and smooth the surface of each with the back of a spoon. Bake for just less than 15 minutes. Remove the cupcakes from the baking tin and place on a wire rack to cool.

6. In the meantime, prepare the frosting. Put all ingredients in a food processor and blend until smooth.

7. Spread a generous layer of frosting on each of the cooled cupcakes.

Recipe 30: Green Tea, Pecan, and Salted Caramel Cupcakes

Baking with green tea is a new trend that is hopefully here to stay. Salted caramel compliments the delicate tea flavors perfectly, and chopped pecans add texture and crunch.

Yield: 12

Preparation Time: 30mins

Total Cooking Time: 25mins

List of Ingredients:

Cupcakes:

- 1½ cups all-purpose flour
- 1 cup granulated sugar
- 1 teaspoon baking soda
- ½ teaspoons salt
- 1 cup almond milk
- ½ cup canola oil
- 2 tablespoons white vinegar
- 1 teaspoon organic vanilla extract

Frosting:

- ½ cup vegan margarine
- ½ cup non-hydrogenated shortening
- 3 cups confectioner's sugar
- ½ teaspoons organic vanilla extract
- 2 tablespoons almond milk
- 1¼ teaspoons green tea powder
- Vegan salted caramel (to drizzle)
- Pecans (finely chopped)

Instructions:

1. Preheat oven to 350 degrees F.

2. In a large bowl, sift together dry ingredients.

3. In a separate bowl, whisk together wet ingredients.

4. Add the dry ingredients to the wet, little by little. Mix until just combined.

5. Fill each cupcake case with the mixture until 2/3 full and smooth the surface of each with the back of a spoon. Bake for just less than 25 minutes. Remove the cupcakes from the baking tin and place on a wire rack to cool.

6. Use an electric mixer to cream together shortening and margarine. Add in remaining ingredients, excluding almond milk. Mix in the milk a little at a time, to control the consistency of frosting.

7. Pipe cooled cupcakes with frosting and decorate with a sprinkling of pecans.

Chapter IV - Over 21s

Cupcakes

AAAAAAAAAAAAAAAAAAAAAAAAAAAAAAAAAAAAAAAAAAAAAAA

Recipe 31: Tiramisu Cupcakes

A new way to enjoy this classic Italian dessert. Amaretto Mascarpone frosting is the perfect decadent topping for the coffee liquor-soaked sponge.

Yield: 24

Preparation Time: 45mins

Total Cooking Time: 23mins

List of Ingredients:

Cupcakes:

- ¾ cup butter
- 1¾ cups sugar
- 3 medium eggs
- 3 tablespoons vanilla
- 1 cup milk
- 2¾ cups all-purpose flour
- 2½ teaspoons baking powder
- ¾ teaspoons salt

Soak:

- 2 tablespoons espresso powder
- 3 tablespoons coffee liquor
- 3 tablespoons sugar
- ¾ cup water (hot)

Frosting:

- 2 cups cream
- ⅔ cup powdered sugar
- 1 cup Mascarpone cheese
- ½ cup amaretto liquor

AAAAAAAAAAAAAAAAAAAAAAAAAAAAAAAAAAAAAAAAAAAA

Instructions:

1. Preheat the oven to 350 degrees F.

2. Beat butter and sugar together. Add in the eggs one by one at a time, mixing well after each addition. Add the vanilla and milk.

3. Sift in the dry ingredients and fold to combine.

4. Fill each cupcake case with the mixture until 3/4 full and smooth the surface of each with the back of a spoon. Bake for approximately 23 minutes, until they are golden brown and spring to the touch. Remove the cupcakes from the baking tin and place on a wire rack to cool.

5. For the soak, mix the espresso, liquor, sugar, and hot water. Pierce each cupcake with a fork and brush with the coffee soak.

6. Make the whipped cream frosting. Whip the cream, powdered sugar, cheese, and amaretto until the mixture is light and fluffy.

7. Pipe the cooled cupcakes with a swirl of the whipped cream.

Recipe 32: Cosmopolitan Cupcakes

A recipe Carrie Bradshaw would approve of. With cranberries soaked in vodka, these boozy cupcakes will liven up any party.

Yield: 24

Preparation Time: 8h 30mins

Total Cooking Time: 25mins

List of Ingredients:

Cranberry mix:

- 1 cup cranberries (dried)
- 1 cup vodka
- ¼ cup triple sec
- One lime, juiced and zested

Cupcakes:

- 3 cups flour
- 3 teaspoons baking powder
- 5 cups confectioner's sugar (sifted)
- 1 teaspoon salt
- 2 cups granulated sugar
- 1 cup unsalted butter (room temperature)
- 4 medium eggs
- 1½ teaspoons vanilla
- ½ teaspoons orange extract
- 1 teaspoon cream of tartar
- 1 cup whole milk

Frosting:

- ½ ounce butter
- ½ teaspoons orange extract
- 1½ teaspoons vanilla extract
- 2 tablespoons cranberry cordial
- 1 tablespoon vodka
- 1 tablespoon triple sec
- 1 tablespoon milk
- Pink food gel
- Corn syrup

AAAAAAAAAAAAAAAAAAAAAAAAAAAAAAAAAAAAAAAAAAAAAAA

Instructions:

1. Start by preparing the cranberry mixture. Blend all ingredients in a food processor and allow to rest overnight.

2. For the cupcakes, sift all dry ingredients into a bowl.

3. In a separate bowl, beat together sugar and butter. Mix in the eggs and beat. Follow that with the orange and vanilla extracts and then the cranberry mixture.

4. Add the dry ingredients to the wet, a little at a time alternating with milk. Take care not to overmix.

5. Fill each cupcake case with the mixture until 2/3 full and smooth the surface of each with the back of a spoon. Bake for just over 20 minutes. Remove the cupcakes from the baking tin and place on a wire rack to cool.

6. In the meantime, prepare the frosting. Use a standing mixer to break up the butter. Add in the remaining ingredients, excluding the confectioner's sugar and beat.

7. Add the confectioner's sugar in, a little at a time remembering to stop to scrape the bottom and sides of the mixing bowl. Add the corn syrup and beat for a final 90 seconds.

8. Pipe the cooled cupcakes with the frosting and enjoy!

Recipe 33: Spiced Sangria Cupcakes

A taste of Spanish summer in one bite! In this recipe, Spain's favorite drink is transformed into a fruity spiced cupcake.

Yield: 12

Preparation Time: 30mins

Total Cooking Time: 15mins

List of Ingredients:

Cupcakes:

- 1 box vanilla cake mix
- ½ cup strawberries (finely chopped)
- ½ cup apples (finely chopped)

Buttercream:

- ½ cup shortening
- 1 stick butter (softened)
- 1½ tablespoons orange zest
- 1 teaspoon vanilla
- 1 tablespoon sugar
- 2½ cups confectioner's sugar
- ½ bottle red wine

AAAAAAAAAAAAAAAAAAAAAAAAAAAAAAAAAAAAAAAAAAAAAA

Instructions:

1. Preheat oven to 355 degrees F.

2. Prepare the cake mix according to packet instructions.

3. Fold the fruit into the cake mix.

4. Fill each cupcake case with the mixture until 3/4 full and smooth the surface of each with the back of a spoon. Bake for approximately 15 minutes, until they are golden brown and spring to the touch. Remove the cupcakes from the baking tin and place on a wire rack to cool.

5. In the meantime, prepare the buttercream. Reduce the red wine in a saucepan over high heat, until it is syrupy and thick. Take off the heat and set to one side.

6. Use an electric whisk, to combine the shortening, butter, orange zest, vanilla, and wine. Slowly add in the confectioner's sugar and whisk until fluffy and light.

7. Pipe the cooled cupcakes with buttercream.

Recipe 34: Gin and Tonic Cupcakes

These sophisticated gin and tonic cupcakes are complimented with flavors of lime and mint. There has never been a tastier way to enjoy an afternoon G&T.

Yield: 12

Preparation Time: 15mins

Total Cooking Time: 25mins

List of Ingredients:

Cupcakes:

- 1 ½ cups self-raising flour
- ¾ ounce plain flour
- 1 teaspoon baking powder
- 1 ½ cups caster sugar
- 1 ½ sticks butter (unsalted)
- 3 small eggs
- 1 teaspoon vanilla
- 3 tablespoons tonic water
- 2 tablespoons gin
- 1 lime (zested)

Frosting:

- 4 cups icing sugar
- 2 ½ sticks unsalted butter
- Milk

AAAAAAAAAAAAAAAAAAAAAAAAAAAAAAAAAAAAAAAAAAAAAA

Instructions:

1. Preheat oven to 360 degrees F.

2. Sift the dry ingredients together into a bowl.

3. Cream the sugar and butter in a bowl using an electric whisk. Add the eggs, beating the mix well after adding each one.

4. Add the dry ingredients to the wet, little by little. Stir in the tonic.

5. Fill each cupcake case with mixture until 2/3 full and smooth the surface of each with the back of a spoon. Bake for approximately 23 to 25 minutes, until they are golden brown and spring to the touch. Use a fork to pierce each cupcake and brush each with gin, until only half of the gin is remaining. Remove the cupcakes from the baking tin and place on a wire rack to cool.

6. In the meantime, prepare the frosting. Whisk together the icing sugar and butter then add what is left of the gin. Use a drop of milk if the icing is too thick.

7. Pipe each of the cooled cupcakes with frosting and decorate with a slice of lime and a sprig of mint.

Recipe 35: Rum and Raisin

Spiced rum is perfect for baking- its caramel and cinnamon undertones add real depth of flavor to these boozy cupcakes. Rum-soaked raisins provide bursts of flavor throughout the sponge.

Yield: 12

Preparation Time: 8h 15mins

Total Cooking Time: 25mins

List of Ingredients:

Cupcakes:

- 1 ¼ cups raisins
- 3 tablespoons dark spiced rum
- 1 ½ cups unsalted butter (softened)
- 3 medium eggs
- 1 ½ cups brown sugar
- 1 teaspoon vanilla
- 2 tablespoons milk
- 1 ½ cups self-raising flour
- 1 ½ teaspoons cinnamon

Whipped Cream Topping:

- 1 ¼ cups double cream
- 1 teaspoon vanilla
- 2 tablespoons powdered sugar

AAAAAAAAAAAAAAAAAAAAAAAAAAAAAAAAAAAAAAAAAAAAAAAA

Instructions:

1. Place the raisins and rum in a sealable container and allow to soak overnight.

2. Preheat oven to 320 degrees F.

3. Cream the butter and sugar until whipped and light.

4. Beat in the eggs, vanilla, and milk.

5. Fold in the flour, a little at a time and then add in the raisins and cinnamon.

6. Fill each cupcake case with the mixture until 2/3 full and smooth the surface of each with the back of a spoon. Bake for approximately 25 minutes, until they are golden brown and spring to the touch. Remove the cupcakes from the baking tin and place on a wire rack to cool.

7. To make the topping, whip together the cream, vanilla, and powdered sugar until the mixture is firm enough to swirl onto the cooled cupcakes. Decorate with any remaining raisins.

Recipe 36: Colleen's Irish Coffee Cupcakes

Thanks to Colleen O'Reilly of NYC for sharing with us her family's St. Patricks Day Irish Coffee cupcake recipe. The whiskey-spiked frosting is the perfect topping for moist espresso and brown sugar sponge.

Yield: 15

Preparation Time: 15mins

Total Cooking Time: 20-25mins

List of Ingredients:

Cupcakes:

- ¼ teaspoons salt
- 2 cups all-purpose flour
- ¼ teaspoons baking soda
- 1 teaspoon baking powder
- 2 tablespoons instant powdered espresso
- ½ cup water (boiling)
- ¼ cup milk
- 1 stick butter (unsalted, room temperature)
- ½ cup brown sugar
- 2 medium eggs

Frosting:

- 1 tablespoon powdered sugar
- 1 cup cream
- 1 tablespoon whiskey
- Instant powdered espresso (for dusting)

AAAAAAAAAAAAAAAAAAAAAAAAAAAAAAAAAAAAAAAAAAAAAA

Instructions:

1. Preheat oven to 350 degrees F.

2. Sift together salt, flour, and baking soda and powder.

3. Make an espresso using the powder and hot water, mix with milk.

4. Cream the butter and sugar. Add in the eggs, one at a time, and mix continuously.

5. Fold in the flour in 3 parts, alternating with additions of coffee mixture.

6. Fill each cupcake case with the mixture until 3/4 full and smooth the surface of each with the back of a spoon. Bake for approximately 23 to 25 minutes, until they are golden brown and spring to the touch. Remove the cupcakes from the baking tin and place on a wire rack to cool.

7. In the meantime, prepare the frosting. Whisk the powdered sugar and cream together. When peaks form, pour in the whiskey and mix until the frosting is stiff.

8. Top each cooled cake with a generous layer or frosting and decorate with a light dusting of espresso powder.

Recipe 37: Pink Champagne Cupcakes

The ultimate celebration cupcake. Pretty pink sponge topped with super airy whipped cream frosting is sure to add glitz and glamor to any special occasion.

Yield: 24

Preparation Time: 15mins

Total Cooking Time: 17mins

List of Ingredients:

Cupcakes:

- 1¾ granulated sugar
- 12 tablespoons unsalted butter
- 6 egg whites
- 1 teaspoon vanilla
- Pink food gel
- 3 cups cake flour
- 1½ teaspoons baking powder
- ¾ teaspoons baking soda
- ¼ teaspoons salt
- 1½ cups champagne

Whipped Cream:

- 2 cups heavy cream
- ¼ cup powdered sugar

AAAAAAAAAAAAAAAAAAAAAAAAAAAAAAAAAAAAAAAAAAAAAA

Instructions:

1. Cream together sugar and butter. Add in the egg whites, vanilla, and food gel until the batter is a pale rose pink.

2. Sift the dry ingredients into the wet stirring continuously.

3. Slowly pour in the champagne and whisk until just combined.

4. Fill each cupcake case with the mixture until 1/2 full and smooth the surface of each with the back of a spoon. Bake for approximately 17 minutes, until they are golden brown and spring to the touch. Remove the cupcakes from the baking tin and place on a wire rack to cool.

5. In the meantime, whip the cream and powdered sugar until it forms stiff peaks.

6. Swirl the whipped cream on the cooled cupcakes.

Recipe 38: Margarita Cupcakes

This recipe comes all the way from a boutique bakery in Miami, Florida. Tequila-soaked lime sponge and frosting sprinkled with coarse salt, definitely adults-only!

Yield: 12

Preparation Time: 3h 20mins

Total Cooking Time: 20mins

List of Ingredients:

Cupcakes:

- 1½ cups all-purpose flour
- 2 teaspoons baking powder
- ½ teaspoons salt
- ½ ounce unsalted butter (room temperature)
- 1 cup sugar
- 2 medium eggs
- 2 teaspoons vanilla extract
- 2 tablespoons tequila
- Zest and juice of 3 limes
- ½ cup milk

Frosting:

- 4 cups powdered sugar
- ½ ounce unsalted butter (room temperature)
- 4 tablespoons tequila
- 2 teaspoons lime extract
- 1 teaspoon vanilla extract
- Salt

AAAAAAAAAAAAAAAAAAAAAAAAAAAAAAAAAAAAAAAAAAAAAAA

Instructions:

1. Preheat oven 350 degrees F.

2. Sift together the dry ingredients and place to one side.

3. Beat all of the wet ingredients together in a large bowl. Stop at intervals to scrape the sides and bottom of the bowl.

4. Mix the dry ingredients into the wet ingredients in 3 batches, alternating each addition with an addition of milk. Mix well, then add the lime juice and zest. Give a final mix until just incorporated.

5. Fill each cupcake case with the mixture until 2/3 full and smooth the surface of each with the back of a spoon. Bake for approximately 20 minutes, until they are golden brown and spring to the touch. Use a fork to pierce each cupcake and brush each with tequila, until only half of the tequila is remaining. Remove the cupcakes from the baking tin and place on a wire rack to cool.

6. In the meantime, prepare the frosting. Whisk the powdered sugar and butter together. Once combined, add the tequila, lime, vanilla, and a pinch of the salt mix until light and creamy.

7. Top each cooled cake with a generous layer or frosting and decorate with a light sprinkling of coarse salt.

Recipe 39: Pina Colada Cupcakes

A medley of pineapple, coconut, and rum. So, if you like Pina Coladas (getting caught in the rain is optional) then try this recipe immediately.

Yield: 18

Preparation Time:

Total Cooking Time: 25mins

List of Ingredients:

Cupcakes:

- ½ cup coconut milk
- ¼ cup cream of coconut
- ⅓ cup dark rum
- 1 teaspoon vanilla extract
- ¼ cup pineapple juice
- 1½ cups all-purpose flour
- 1½ teaspoons salt
- ½ stick unsalted butter (softened)
- 1 cup white sugar
- 3 tablespoons brown sugar
- 3 medium eggs
- 2 cups crushed pineapple
- 1 cup shredded coconut

Buttercream:

- 1 cup butter (room temperature)
- 4 ½ cups powdered sugar
- 1 tablespoon coconut milk
- 1 tablespoon cream of coconut
- 1 tablespoon dark rum
- 1 teaspoon vanilla extract

AAAAAAAAAAAAAAAAAAAAAAAAAAAAAAAAAAAAAAAAAAAA

Instructions:

1. Preheat oven to 350 degrees F.

2. Combine the coconut milk and cream, rum, vanilla, and pineapple juice. Set to one side.

3. Sift together the dry ingredients and add in the butter a little at a time. Then add the wet ingredient mixture and the eggs one at a time, beating after each addition.

4. Fold in the pineapple and coconut until just combined.

5. Fill each cupcake case with the mixture until 3/4 full and smooth the surface of each with the back of a spoon. Bake for approximately 23 to 25 minutes, until they are golden brown and spring to the touch. Remove the cupcakes from the baking tin and place on a wire rack to cool.

6. In the meantime, prepare the buttercream. Use an electric mixer to cream the butter. Add the powdered sugar in batches until all combined. Add the coconut milk, cream, rum, and vanilla until the buttercream is light and fluffy.

7. Frost the cooled cupcakes with the buttercream ad decorate with a sprinkling of flaked coconut.

Recipe 40: Mojito Cupcakes

Packed with powerful, fresh flavors. The secret to these boozy cupcakes is 'bruising' the mint leaves before adding them to the batter, to release their fragrant oil.

Yield: 12

Preparation Time: 45mins

Total Cooking Time: 25mins

List of Ingredients:

Cupcakes:

- ½ cup fresh mint (bruised)
- ½ cup buttermilk
- 1½ cups all-purpose flour
- 1½ teaspoons baking powder
- ¼ teaspoons salt
- 1 cup unsalted butter (softened)
- 1 cup sugar
- 2 medium eggs
- Juice and zest of 2 limes
- 2 tablespoons white rum
- ¼ teaspoons vanilla

For Soaking:

- 2 tablespoons white rum
- 2 whole sprigs mint

Frosting:

- 1½ cups unsalted butter (softened)
- 4¼ cups confectioner's sugar
- 1½ tablespoons fresh lime juice
- 3 tablespoons white rum

AAAAAAAAAAAAAAAAAAAAAAAAAAAAAAAAAAAAAAAAAAAAA

Instructions:

1. Preheat oven to 325 degrees F.

2. Over medium heat, combine ½ cup of mint and buttermilk in a saucepan. Steam, but don't bring to a simmer. Take off the heat, set to one side and cover for 30 minutes.

3. Strain the mint/milk mixture into a small bowl, whisk lightly until no lumps remain and set aside.

4. Combine the dry ingredients in a large mixing bowl.

5. In a separate bowl whisk, together the wet ingredients (excluding the lime zest and juice, rum, and vanilla). Stop at intervals to scrape down the bottom and sides of the bowl.

6. Add in the remaining wet ingredients and stir until just combined, taking care not to over mix.

7. Add the dry ingredients to the wet, alternating each addition of flour with an addition of the infused buttermilk.

8. Fill each cupcake case with the mixture until 3/4 full and smooth the surface of each with the back of a spoon. Bake for approximately 23 to 25 minutes, until they are golden brown and spring to the touch. Remove the cupcakes from the baking tin and place on a wire rack to cool.

9. In the meantime, warm the rum and mint sprigs in a pan over medium heat. Do not allow to reach a simmer. Take off the heat and set aside while you prepare the frosting. After the cupcakes have been cooling for 10 minutes, brush each with the mint/rum mixture.

10. To prepare the frosting, use an electric mixer to beat together the butter and confectioner's sugar for 5 minutes. Add the rum and lime juice and whisk until light and airy.

11. Pipe the cooled cupcakes with the frosting.

About the Author

Molly Mills always knew she wanted to feed people delicious food for a living. Being the oldest child with three younger brothers, Molly learned to prepare meals at an early age to help out her busy parents. She just seemed to know what spice went with which meat and how to make sauces that would dress up the blandest of pastas. Her creativity in the kitchen was a blessing to a family where money was tight and making new meals every day was a challenge.

Molly was also a gifted athlete as well as chef and secured a Lacrosse scholarship to Syracuse University. This was a blessing to her family as she was the first to go to college and at little cost to her parents. She took full advantage of her college education and earned a business degree. When she graduated, she joined her culinary skills and business acumen into a successful catering business. She wrote her first e-book after a customer asked if she could pay for several of her recipes. This sparked the entrepreneurial spirit in Mills and she thought if one person wanted them, then why not share the recipes with the world!

Molly lives near her family's home with her husband and three children and still cooks for her family every chance she gets. She plays Lacrosse with a local team made up of her old teammates from college and there are always some tasty nibbles on the ready after each game.

Don't Miss Out!

Scan the QR-Code below and you can sign up to receive emails whenever Molly Mills publishes a new book. There's no charge and no obligation.

Sign Me Up

https://molly.gr8.com

Printed in Great Britain
by Amazon